Chasing Fireflies

Erin Nicole

to you

my truth seekers

may you

always

stay

chasing

the light

what you want was
placed within your heart
long before your first breath

you are a flame
no wind or water
can put out

Chasing Fireflies
copyright © 2019 by Erin Nicole

All rights reserved.
No part of this book may be used or reproduced in any matter whatsoever without written permission except in the case of reprints in the context of reviews.

@xoerinnicole on Instagram

Editor: Chloe Winstanley
Book Design & Layout: Lisa Von De Linde

ISBN: 978-0-578-52484-9

TABLE OF CONTENTS

chasing

{5}

discovering

{73}

flying

{127}

we all want
to be accepted
so, we hide our faces
while our hearts cry
to be seen

I was a dancer
you were a dreamer
round and round
back and forth
we flowed

even if
tonight
is all we ever have
you will always have
tiny pieces of my
heart
please carry them with you
and hold them tight

let's pack our bags
you and I
do best
in open spaces

there was so much
love between
hello and goodbye

and we crashed
against each other
like the sand and the sea
leaving both of us undone

heart of a dreamer
soul of a gypsy
I can't seem to stay
for too long
floating and running
in flux with the wind

CHASING FIREFLIES

I met you and my
heart crackled
like dry firewood
unfamiliar with
the heat and flame
that would later
turn to ashes
another musky
scent of
a love that
flickered out

you are the storm
and wind to my sail

CHASING FIREFLIES

I lay here
as you speak
to my heart
promising me the stars
never once
giving me the sky
|empty promises

my eyes always
spoke the truths
that my mouth found
difficult to bear

CHASING FIREFLIES

                we ran around
                chasing after
                fallen stars
            and runaway hearts
            hoping to make them
                    ours
                trying to catch
                    love
                in a glass jar
            |chasing fireflies

I wrote our story
on the page
so it would
never have to die

love only hurts
when you try to
make it yours

I have been
losing you
over and over
again
each day
I wake up
hoping for a
different truth

with you I
aimed to please
always down
on my knees
begging you not
to forget me

I just feel
like our love
can save us
|some lies live on

you have been
holding on
so tightly
to the broken pieces
that you didn't
even notice
the blood
dripping
down

our love couldn't
last
forever
even the great
walls
fall down

If only our
worlds had never
collided
my heart would
be less
broken
and my eyes
less accustomed
to sin

every night
we swim
in the fire
hoping not
to burn
|life of sin

I take a sip
from you and sway
as I drink myself
drunk
once again

you have
blood
on your hands
but your lips
grace
mine
I let you in
ignoring the
dark crimson
red

I saw the devil
in your eyes
as your carelessly
watched me drown

if I could have only
seen your lies
wrapped in the crumbled
sheets and words
that so eloquently
flowed from your tongue
maybe I wouldn't be here
trying to piece
together our world
and my heart

many evils I have
enjoyed
I'm just an aimless soul
hoping this one
won't be the
end

I open my mouth
and swallow my soul
as you take another
breathe of mine
my lungs
cry for air
but my body
screams for your touch
the war
I endure
just to feel
your love

I am sure you don't
even notice me
starting to change
like the leaves on
the trees
you will only
miss me
when I am gone

the city lights
make me think of you
how they twinkle
and dance
begging me to play again
with a fire
that is extinguished
in the early
morning light

CHASING FIREFLIES

you tore my
walls
down
grabbed my
heart
and
tossed it
to the wayside
|trash

you are forever
imprinted
in my heart
no matter
how many times
I die
you beat on

you taught me what it
means to open my heart
to another
and then you showed me
how to close it to the world
you showed me how to be wanted
and how it feels to beg for love
you were who I wanted forever
but you always drew a line
you were never really mine
and now,
not at all
you were who I couldn't live without
and then someone I hated
you didn't stop me when I left
but you wouldn't say goodbye
your love almost killed me
but I am here
still alive

I stood in the driveway
as you poured gasoline
on the fire
while the tears
ran down my face
hoping they could
put it out

people's hearts
don't get recycled
they have to
endure
the decay

I always chose
the worst things
to fall in love with
whiskey, pain
and you

CHASING FIREFLIES

you were once
my air
then you left
and took out
my lungs

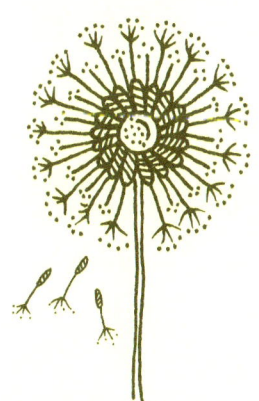

soon I will be
sleeping
in an empty bed
again
begging my heart
to keep me warm

my scars
are proof
that the fire
doesn't scare me

this is the last time
I say
as you place your
lips on mine
my words,
we both know,
are a lie

I wish my tears
were in your eyes
so you could feel
what you did to me

you grab my waist
and whisper
speaking your heart
into the silence
this night will soon
be over
but our eyes
lack wisdom
in the dark

every scar was a
kiss
from your lips
a mistake that I
relished

don't ask to be held
by the very hands
that broke you
|comfort

I thought my
heart knew
darkness
until I found
you

when you walked away
I saw you for the first time
|blind

somehow you know
when I am
happy
you magically
reappear
eager to love
but not to stay
|to love a narcissist

you light a
fire
in me
smile
turn around
and leave

I go down
in flames
|match

he is here tonight
but all I can think about is
the last time your
mouth touched mine
and how many ways
he is not you
but still, I let him stay
because
lying here with your ghost
is too much for
my heart to take
|late night confessions

nothing can come close
to you,
and I am not sure
if that is a
blessing or a
curse

I like to think
there are two
people out there
just like us
that got it right
that is how I
get through
|happy endings

maybe in a few years, our hearts will be
ready to dance together again

CHASING FIREFLIES

if you have to fight
for his love
toss the white flag
and walk away
|I call that a win

it's not my fault
you didn't hear me
when I said goodbye—
this revolving door
no longer
spins
to your
empty kisses
and lies

the pieces that
had to be left behind
will eventually float
into the night sky
so, tonight when you
see the stars
smile in wonder
because they are
part of who
you are

he never should have let you
stay
but that's the
thing—
he wasn't
capable of loving you
how you deserve,
but was too selfish
to allow you to
experience real love
without him

you broke me
in ways no one
can ever understand
and it took years
to build back the
pieces of my shattered heart
so, please know
I really don't care
if you are OK
and no,
I don't want to hear from you
because
you almost killed my light
don't come around here
with your darkness
because I am not
that same timid girl
who is going to let you
back in

I am not sure
if I believe
in all that
I can be
without you
so I stay up
all night
trying to find you
in the sky

I want to go
back to the way
things were
before I met her
she is the sun
and without her
I am just walking
through life
in the dark

can we go
back
to the start
when you
saw me
as I am

he said I need
to leave
I blinked, confused
how can the stars
leave the moon
and not fall
from the sky

I think about
you
every night
as I travel around
this world
he can never
hold me
like you—
pieces of me have gone
missing
I don't know if I will
get them back
my heart got left
in your hands

I am not sure if it's the
breeze
or the
whiskey
that's whispering
sweet sympathies
for me to come
back to you

all that we cling to
is
never meant to stay

when I realized
I was doing the breaking
I was the one in pain
slowly and quickly
falling apart
I realized I had to leave
not so you would no longer hurt me
but so I would finally stop
hurting myself

the only tragedy in
loving a man
who doesn't feel
the same
is
if you stay

every day
I wake up
and have to kill
the old me
that needed
you

I release
pieces of you
with each breath

like stardust,
they dance
before me
enticing my heart

CHASING FIREFLIES

I wanted to stay there
forever
but life didn't work out
that way
so, I hang on
to the love that we
once knew

days go by
each one named
and numbered
until I can barely
remember what made me
love you

I used to think that
love
was a crazy insatiable hunger
for the other
but this only left me empty
and constantly trying to quiet
the pit inside

maybe that love
was supposed to
break us
crack us open
so that we are
more alive and awake
so that we can
feel deeper
live more openly
and fall more madly
in love with
our souls

I ached and cried
for you to love me
but what I needed
was to learn how to
love and accept myself
all of my faults
and shortcomings
and to come
home to my body
and the love
inside my soul

I have enough reasons
to leave
but a million more
to stay
love, save me
I don't want to be
done yet
I have too much
left to give

hang on
girl, stay strong
this feeling won't
last forever
you will move on
I promise
this pain will
leave
all will wash away
girl, stay strong
please just
hang on

I know the world
has tried to
break you
but hold close
to the truth
inside
and do whatever
you need
to stay alive
|we need you here

darling, I know you think
your darkness is too scary
that sometimes you feel
like you can't breathe
that running never
feels far enough
to quiet the ache in your chest
and the monsters
that live in your mind
all you want to do is forget
about all that tried to break you
and all of that damn regret
but I promise you that love
hasn't met a fear she can't beat yet

many nights of this life
I have died
and left pieces of
my gentle soul
behind
trying to make
this world mine

my biggest fear
is giving someone
my heart
and it being shattered
so instead, I shackle her up
and hide away
to watch as I break
her apart

darling, I hope
you can forgive her
the side of me that
tried to do us wrong
turned our life
into rubble
and tried to
kiss this beautiful life
goodbye

who knew a heart
could live for so long
in the cold

And yet here I am. My heart is beating all the same. Maybe a little more cautious than before, but when you see the darkness you will do anything to not go back. Even when the heart breaks, somehow it still beats on.

I sit in the
darkness,
waiting for
the peace
to still my mind,
and heal my
heart

and after it is all over
I hope you remember
the best of your years
are still to come
so, keep your head up,
darling,
as you walk along
or you will miss
the rainbow
once the rain
is gone

it's not whether or not
you will be tested
its whether or not you will
continue to stay
walking on your path

CHASING FIREFLIES

many nights
I heard a noise
calling out to my shadows
to live out the darkness again
but I hold tight
to the glimmer of light
that I have felt even
at my weakest
to bring me back
into the world again

she ran amongst
the horses
a wild heart
that was never
meant to be tamed

CHASING FIREFLIES

your happily ever after
is out there waiting
for you to fall in love
with yourself first
so you will recognize
real love
when you find it

I am but a star
in this world
searching
for my place
in the sky

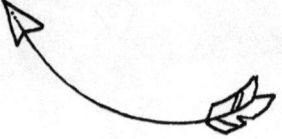

we break, bleed, open
allowing to be touched
and caressed by life

find me a rock
that has been
touched by the sea
and has not been
changed forever

we are all
walking around
with broken hearts
searching for the pieces
we lost along the way
hoping to be
put back together
|broken

I want to go back in time
and hug that scared girl
who was desperately
trying not to lose you
and let her know
the only tragedy in love
is when we lose ourselves

CHASING FIREFLIES

I watched as
you
and all the things I can't change
were washed away
all I ask is
that you ride
the waves
and remember
our love so sweet

most losses don't
disappear
forever
how else would we
create the
stars above
if it weren't
for all the
ones we have
loved
making their way
home

CHASING FIREFLIES

the best gift
you gave me
was bringing me
back to myself
when you let
me go,
I ran back home

in the space of our
deepest suffering
if we are still enough,
the light between us
will guide us back home

I sit in darkness
waiting for the peace
to still my mind
and heal my heart

hold tight to your
belief in the good
I know this world
can be cold at times
but you don't have to be
show them your heart
it is the warmest place
I have ever known

CHASING FIREFLIES

broken tears
and lost fights
weary hearts
and the lies
don't matter
naked as we dance
under the moonlight
lay it all down
and float on
tonight

finally, her eyes saw
what I had all along
and for once in her
life
she left all the
hate
and self-loathing
behind
and met herself
with open arms

I wish I could go back to that scared little girl and tell her it was all going to be OK. That she didn't have to act so brave when deep down she was hurting. That crying doesn't make her weak. That it's OK to give her heart out after it has been hurt. That people are innately good. That it's OK to not have it all figured out. That it's OK to fuck up. That it is OK sometimes to be a complete mess. That it is OK to let someone hold you until you make it through. That she doesn't have to do it all alone. That just maybe we have to break a little before we grow. I wish I could hug her so she knew that she wasn't alone. That we make it. That love is what got us through.

look up to the sky
and see how
you can fly
you are bigger
than all the demons
and all the reasons why
you pull yourself
down
you were meant
for the heavens
to soar in the clouds
you were never meant
to keep both
feet on the ground
|take back your wings

today I walked back
toward her
my essence, my soul
the one I promised
years ago
to never leave behind
my beloved
my one sweet friend

I rose from the ashes
after years
of dancing in your flame
no amount
of madness, love
will take me back

I have found solace
in the arms
of my own love
|I made it without you

he said you look different
I said I know
I no longer need you

These eyes have witnessed all the pains this world has to offer. I have lived through more heart-break than most. I have dabbled with my life and sin. I have let go of all my self-worth and have fought for it back. I have loved so hard and I have been so cold. I have been so confident and the next day not know what the fuck I am doing here. This is life. This is being alive. And I wouldn't trade any of it to not feel again.

I think love is
something that never
has to fade
just put your hand
over your chest
and know you
are love

lay it all down
and surrender
step out of the armor
and be still
my love
let the light
illuminate your soul
|light

she danced around
in circles
to her own song
never once
letting the world
tell her she had
got it wrong

CHASING FIREFLIES

I think the world is holding onto
all the love you freely gave out
until you are able to replicate it
back to yourself
before she is ready to give you
back the love you deserve
then when you are ready
and fully understand
what it means to receive
that's when the greatest love
is going to find you
because there is such a beautiful space
for them to land

our minds
churn
to find
clarity
unable to fathom
the ambiguity
of our
souls

I am not sure
why we have to
endure pain
in this world
all I know is that
we are all still here
and our stories
are the hands
that interlock us

a butterfly must crawl
before gifted
its wings

CHASING FIREFLIES

Flying

wild flowers
grow in the cracks
of time
and between the
love that you
so desperately
had to leave
behind

you will see one day
that all of life
comes and goes
the waves, they fade
and the sun will
no longer burn
and you can endure
the cold
and the memories that
once made you fold
stay rooted
in the truth that you know
let it all come
let it all go

life's gifts
are in the stillness
of the clouds
during our
greatest storms

you will love again
after all the tears
have been shed
and you have been stripped
away of the hurt
and anger and pain
when you feel
you have no more fighting left
that is when love
will find you

we are all
spinning around
in our little worlds
waiting to collide

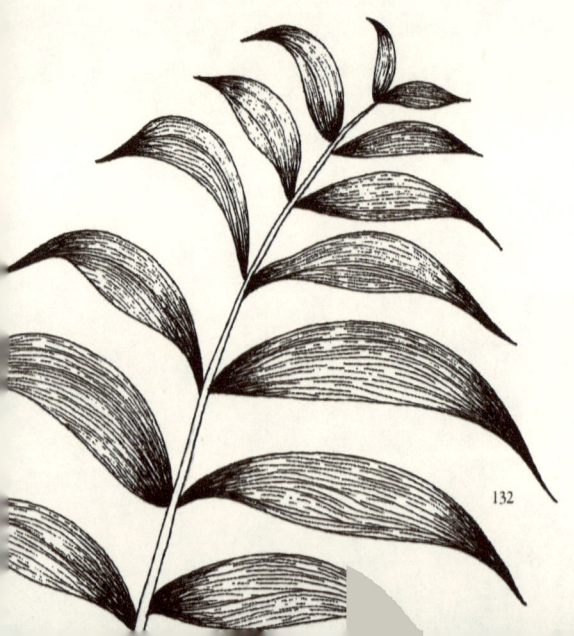

I stopped believing
in accidents long ago
I know now
that our hearts
lead us to where
we are meant to be
always
I know this in my bones
and when you land
in a place
you have been
hoping for
you too will believe
in the power of
the unlimited
because you will feel it
in the depths
of your soul

we are all searching for it
that kiss
that makes the past disappear
the arms that
keep away our fears
the body
that makes ours come alive
the heart
that beats in sync with time
the soul
that recognizes that we are one
love
is why we stay chasing the sun

I slip
in and out
of these dresses
waiting to be
found by you

brick by brick
she built
a wall around
her fragile heart
desperately hoping
one day it could
be knocked down

CHASING FIREFLIES

I don't know you
but it doesn't
keep me from dreaming
of the day we will meet
this is what keeps me
hoping,
and keeps my heart alive
|to my future love

I don't believe in perfect timing. I believe we find who we are meant to in the right time. That person you think was just bad timing was simply the wrong person. They were never meant to stay. The right person will find you when you are both ready. And yes, it may take time, but I promise you that perfect moment is worth it.

a soulmate is not someone who makes you feel whole
—they challenge you to complete yourself.
they stay when others won't.
they aren't afraid of the darkness because they have been there too.
they love all of you, even the parts you want to hide.
in loving you they will constantly push you to grow.
to evolve.
because their job is to make you better.
to make the world better.

walk with me
I will be right
next to you
through the darkness
I will shine
the light on you
when it is too scary
for you to breathe
hand in hand
we will make it
together

I open my heart
and watch as
my fears
begin to fade
high on the clouds
miles away

I have danced
my way around
this world
but nothing
makes me move
like you

CHASING FIREFLIES

when I met you
I knew you were
who I had been
waiting for
all
along
our eyes met
and our souls wept
for all that had gone
wrong

my reflex is always
to run
save him from
my untamed battered
heart

I don't make it easy
to get to my heart
and at times
I can be hard to love
but I just want
that one who isn't
afraid to try

Sometimes I feel too much. And then nothing at all. It's a dance. One I don't always get right. But I promise always to keep swaying and moving towards too much. To keep loving hard. That is one thing that can't be taken away. Our ability to love. Even if it's hard. It is always our choice. Even though I have been broken and have fallen more than I would have liked, I do know that our hearts can always be put back together. Maybe not the same as before. But still whole. And we just have to keep beating on until we find that person who helps us make sense of all that had to go wrong. How we landed here. All I know is that I am glad my heart kept beating. And I kept trusting.

Kept fighting. For love.

your kiss
tasted like
the rain
a promise
to wash anew

show her
that she has gotten
it all wrong
the good ones
stay
just keep loving her

I could stare
at your eyes
forever
they always
take me home

I love the way
your eyes
dance when
you talk about
her

hand and hand
we dance in circles
this love we share
is my only fear

in the rain is always
where I feel you most

some of the softest, most
beautiful souls
have endured the most
heartache and pain
and chose to love anyway

Some of the softest souls have lived through some of the hardest circumstances. They remain kind even in a world that may have been unkind to them. They give their heart to others even after it has been ripped to pieces. They give their love freely because they know what it is like to live in a world without it. That is beauty. That is strength. To show up in this world and love is the bravest thing any of us can do.

it's holding a loved one's hand as they take their last breath
it's shutting the door and not turning back
it's making the tough call alone at the bar
it's saying no when it is so much easier to say yes
it's walking away from everything that you built
because it no longer makes sense to you
it's telling someone you love them knowing they might not feel the same
it's picking up that paintbrush after your showing flopped
it's taking a year off to travel
it's feeling your heart break and allowing it to open again to this magical life
this is what it means to be brave
this is what it means to be alive
|brave

you deserve someone
who is easy like Sunday mornings
and makes your heart beat
like early spring

tonight I sat
across from
him and knew
every heartbreak
was worth it

I long for the night
so I can close my eyes
and feel you
and know I am
no longer alone

fly away with me
amongst the clouds
away from the noise
let go of the world
darling,
and come dance
with the stars

I wish I could reach
past the stars,
grab the moon
and bring her down
so she wasn't
so far
so you could feel
her too

her eyes pierced you with truth
an unwavering glance
she saw you
and you recognized she was it
that moment you knew
you would risk everything
to be hers forever
|the one

I hope you fall
in love
a million times
over this life
with her

close your eyes
and forget
your troubles
stay with me
for awhile
in the heart
of this song

CHASING FIREFLIES

you are the purest soul
that I have known
my whole life
and I will wait
for you
until the night
says good bye
to the stars
before I let
you out of my arms

I hope he tells you
you are beautiful
in the morning
and kisses you hard
at the end of the day
holds your hand
and chases all
the monsters away

you grab me
from behind
and pull me close
kissing my neck
caressing my skin
taking me
by the hand
and I fall back
in love all
over again

love is a glance
of eternity
in the eyes
of another

the power of love
is within the heat of the flame
that pumps the life back into my veins
when our flesh is entangled
and our lips are locked
hearts beating as one
together burning
hotter than the sun

CHASING FIREFLIES

our heartbeats
entwined like the
sand and sea
our love bound
like the moon and me
together for
eternity

I could never see
the sun's golden light
until it was
reflecting off your face
I never truly saw
the beauty of the wind
until it was blowing
your hair in disarray
I never understood
the strength of the earth
until you kissed me
and my knees gave out
I never understood
the heat of the fire until
your skin was on mine
and I never understood
the depths of beauty
until you captured my heart

don't you see
there is a little
bit of heaven
in everyone
just keep your head
tilted towards the sun

how can you
witness the magic
of the stars
and the beat of our
love
and not believe in
eternity

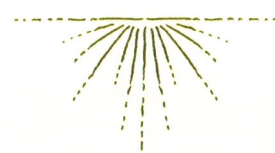

it's in your eyes
and in the smile
that follows
that I know
I will be held
by your love
forever

I want to live

forever

and a day

so I never

have to live

without

you

our love
is the last
story
I care to write

I want the sun
to be the first thing
and the last thing I see
and I want to be
holding your hand
when I don't make it
through the night

we didn't find
each other
there were
pieces of you
in me
all along

Little girl, do you remember? When you would sit and stare up to the clouds. When you would play in the grass. Spin around laughing, not caring if you fell down. You knew the world would catch you. She was your playground. The stars were your map. Your heart your only compass You gave out hugs and kisses freely. You bowed for your own show. Why, child, did you stop being you? Dancing naked in the light. Singing out of tune. Come back, sweet child, we need more of you.

don't let this world
tell you
who or what to be
where to place your
values
or prove your worth
girl, you were made
from gold
sent to this earth
to spread your love
like fairy dust

Do you ever wonder what your life would be like if you turned left instead of right? What she would be like—the girl who decided to do things just a little bit different. Who didn't go to college. Who didn't care so much about proving herself in this world and just freely followed her heart. Listening only to her gentle heartbeats and never hearing all the outside noise. Who didn't try to find solace in boys and took a little extra care of her own sweet soul. Who spent hours lost in nature and the simple wonders of this earth. Who cared less about her beauty and more about creating it. Who maybe spent too much time in the sun and cared very little about her hair that always seemed to be astray. Who stayed up too late dancing and inviting strangers out to play. I am not sure what made me leave that girl behind when I turned right, but even if it takes my whole life, I will find her.

don't look to
the sky
in wonder
you too
were made in
the clouds

if I knew today
was goodbye
I would have told you
the million reasons why
I want to stay
and how grateful
I am to be alive
and how much
I love the simple beat
of a song
and to see the sun
after she has been gone
for so long
to stare at the stars
and be held tightly in your arms
I would give anything
to not leave
oh, how I wish I could stay
please love don't waste
your life away

sometimes I close
my eyes
just so I can feel
what it is like
to fly

CHASING FIREFLIES

there is only one
way into the
kingdom of heaven
that is to live
as if
we are already
there

you will never
be here again
this kiss
will be your last
this dance
your one
and only
life is full
of these
small moments
that will never happen
the same way
again

life constantly
sends us reminders
to believe
to love
to live
just keep your eyes
up and open

I sat across from her
and listened as she told me
about life and love
about the heartaches and triumphs
and the memories
she would not get to share
and then she looked at me
and told me the truest of words
we all struggle here to find our way
lean into the people closest
to you
they were sent here
to help you along the way
never give up on yourself
and always be grateful
that you get to be here
We all don't get the same number of trips around the sun.
Always be grateful.

one day,
you, too, will know
that all that tried
to break you
is the very thing
that will make you
shine

when we live
infinitely as we
were created
we can't help but
fly
amongst the stars
and float along
like the sea

I know it feels like I left you
like I'm miles away
but I'm here
in all the beauty you see
in your heart beat
just be quiet and feel
the love inside
and around
and know that I am
with you
forever and always

I hope you never stop
tasting the wonders
of this world
I hope you never
stop believing in magic
and everyday miracles
the power of the infinite
and the God within us all

even as the music
fades
I hope you
keep swaying
to your own song

When we let go expectations of what and who we should be,
then we are free to be who we are. A divine creative being sent here
to create and love without limitations. Without boundaries.
Outside the confines of our minds and within the infinity of our hearts.
This is who we really are. Remarkable beyond our own existence.
An illuminated light sent to shine love on the world.

CHASING FIREFLIES

I am spinning
in circles
floating
with the spirits
dancing with the souls
that too know
love is what
is taking us
all home

I hope you never stop being in awe of this world's beauty. I hope you live a life of wonder. A life of imagination. A life of creation. This world needs more art, more music, more souls that have been set on fire. That haven't been silenced by this world. That aren't afraid to do what it takes for their own evolution. That want to leave this world a better place.

I hope you stay
exactly as you are
in love
with the stars
with the gentle beat
within your heart
and with all of the beauty
that you are

CHASING FIREFLIES

and so, we go out
searching incessantly
for the light
capturing fireflies
in hand
and the magic
that they bring
to the darkness of night
with hopes
that their illumination
will bring us back
home

you

are

the light

the love

the truth

you have been

chasing

-welcome home

ABOUT THE AUTHOR

Erin Nicole is a poet, writer, yoga teacher, nurse, and forever truth seeker and chaser of the light. She resides in a small town in Pennsylvania. When she is not writing or healing, you can find her lost in the woods. *Chasing Fireflies* is her debut poetry collection.

Website: www.xoerinnicole.com
Instagram: @xoerinnicole

www.ingramcontent.com/pod-product-compliance
Lightning Source LLC
Chambersburg PA
CBHW021406290426
44108CB00010B/402